A Book About Books

Daniel Lisi

OBF Book Publishers
Los Angeles, CA

For information, contact daniel@lisi.website

Paperback ISBN: 979-8-9904865-0-8
eBook ISBN: 979-8-9904865-1-5

Cover Design by Shaun Roberts
Edited by Sam Austen

www.lisi.website

Table of Contents

For Z. Thank you for granting us your gifts, your power, a reverberation that will be felt forever.

FOREWORD

"I found that literature, like all religions,
is also a business."

– Jason Epstein, Book Business

Festina lente, latin for *make haste slowly*, is represented in the logo of publisher Doubleday Books; a dolphin (agile, lithe) curling itself around an anchor (cold, grounding). What a perfect thing to say about what a publisher does—make haste, *slowly*.

Every step in the process of making a book is slow, but the cerebral and market pressures surrounding the act of publishing demands agility. Distributors command seasonal catalogs from their publishers, editors keep their authors to their deadlines, and authors are in concert with whatever demon is coaxing them along their own twisted and alchemical process.

In cultural industries we are constantly balancing and often at odds between the realities of making art (space, time, meandering) and patronizing art (capital, market, audience). This balance has seen dramatic moments of accelerated change from the days of Doubleday in its establishment in 1897 to today's online-induced rapidity.

Doubleday Books is now the Knopf Doubleday Publishing Group, a division of Penguin Random House, a part of the Bertelsmann global media conglomerate; a company that holds a little over 10% of the US book trade. In 2023, Penguin Random House released approximately 20,000 new books across its imprints.

Legendary book publisher Jason Epstein, formerly of Doubleday, witnessed the change of publisher priorities when Doubleday was purchased by Penguin and subsequently opened up for an IPO. He remarks in his book *Book Business* of the shift in the company's priorities from *editor interests* to *shareholder interests*. Today we are witnessing more shifts in priorities as many of Epstein's predictions have come to fruition since his seminal title released in 2001. Accelerationism fueled by capital, communication technology, and corporate consolidation has created an entirely new landscape for publishers and authors to contend with. The dolphin has abandoned the anchor.

* * *

This book brings together roughly ten years of lessons in developing literary programs, from building new publishing houses to deploying post-graduate classes on the business of books. A constellation of workshops, pitfalls, and successes inform this slim volume. The content is largely skewed toward the high level business components of book publishing, with some interjections on aesthetics, marketing, and *vibes*.

Readers will walk away with a better understanding of how the business of books functions from first principles—the underlying supply chain of the trade-released book from concept to bookstore shelf. Authors will gain insight on the financial realities behind making a title *available anywhere books are sold*, what separates quality independent labels and Big Five labels alike, and things to think about when seeking a publisher. For those who want to work in publishing there is useful information to be found with entry-level application, along with some universal fundamentals for those looking to build their own publishing company or simply enrich their understanding.

Today, publishers are all faced with a similar fundamental problem: balancing cash flow. It's common to throw the margins of books under the bus when scrutinizing book publishing as a business, but cashflow is the killer culprit: fixed costs with staff, variable upfront costs with print manufacturing, and typical quarter-long delays in receiving revenue. These capital-intensive realities demand *hits*, which are far more difficult to engineer in today's saturated content market. The valley between titles that sell hundreds of units and those that sell tens of thousands of units is immense; it's estimated that 1-2% of titles sell over 10,000 copies within their first year, with an estimated 70-80% selling under 1,000 units.

Compared to other media businesses, 10,000 units is a relatively small number, but an immense milestone in books across genres. All publishers are under pressure to sustain dealflow with titles that meet sales expectations, needing killer accuracy on their catalog planning to ensure proper cashflow management. This requires creative strategy when dealing with today's distributors and wholesalers; parts of the supply chain that are over a decade behind the times. Let's say it here first: distribution is a massive source of today's problems in the book business, and as such, a big vector for disruption. This theme is a constant throughline in this book.

Why this book, why now? I feel like we haven't received a proper book on the business of books since Jason Epstein's *Book Business* in 2001. I love that book, and I recommend you read it. Epstein's book is important because it gives readers an understanding of how we got to today's consolidation of everything, a phenomenon that is not unique to book publishing. He lived through Random House becoming Penguin Random House and going public, the results of priorities skewing from privately held interests to shareholders. Epstein also predicted Ingram's moves on two fronts; a consolidation in distribution and print on demand.

Print on demand and online e-commerce technologies together have fundamentally changed the behavior of books over the last decade by radically democratizing key components of publishing. There are upsides and downsides to this, the boons and ramifications experienced in real time. This book is a representation of this very disruption, having been self-published via my self-publishing imprint designed to take advantage of the suite of global e-commerce and automated print platforms that now exist. There is no easier time than today to fully conceptualize and deliver on a book, but know that you're competing against approximately 7,000 to 15,000 new title uploads *a day* across leading self-publishing platforms.

I have spent the better part of a decade contending with the problems I call out in *A Book About Books*;

problems publishers, authors, and all who are concerned with the state of literature face. Potentially one day we will work on solving these problems together, or you will exceed me in my own competitive path. I wrote this book for three reasons: to act as a compression algorithm for my partners, to encapsulate all of my class material, and to keep my own writing practice sharp. I am excited to share the results with you, reader. Herein we lower the opacity on how this all works and inspire something in you to go out and build.

I

PROBLEMS

Problems are inevitable and I don't perceive them as *bad*. They are a product of our crawling state of entropy. The thrilling part is that we have the opportunity to harness a problem like a wild stallion and ride it directly into the sun. Let's mount our stallion by taking a high-level look at each step of the supply chain and the problems that exist within them. Bold phrases are industry terms that have been expanded upon in the glossary, starting on page 102.

PROBLEMS WITH BIG PUBLISHING

Book publishing has been severely disrupted by print on demand and the democratization of distribution that it has granted independent authors. Social media amplifies this effect by providing individuals with large followings more **distribution capital** than publishers. Today, publisher acquisitions are less influenced by curatorial tastemaking and behave more like venture capital—in other words, the logic is to purchase assets below their value, corner a market or genre, cast a wide net, and hope for some whales.

As such, book publishers have become increasingly averse to risk and more prone to homogenized choices; taking obvious bets, following trends in lieu of being "ahead of the curve," and shirking anything too "avant-garde." What I largely mean by this is book publishers have flattened their content considerations into a predictable pancake and invest far less in evangelizing new talent.

The data that emerged from the U.S. Department of Justice's antitrust suit filed in 2021 against Penguin Random House (Bertelsmann) over its attempted acquisition of Simon & Schuster from Paramount Global reveal the following trends:

> 1. Emerging to mid-career talent are being largely ignored; author care *can* be great but has great potential to be stagnant. Of 14,000 PRH titles published in 2021, 90% sold under 1,000 copies.
> 2. Advances are shrinking, even for authors who have previously published bestsellers. The consolidated market has reduced competition between big publishers, driving down advances.

3. Criteria in assessing emerging talent has changed to fit a fast-paced churn of content informed by social media and parasocial clout.

PROBLEMS WITH DISTRIBUTORS

Throughout this book I detail the **'Book Trade'**— the ecosystem of distributors, wholesalers, and booksellers that are all responsible for the movement of books and how companies like Ingram and Amazon are entrenched across several crucial layers of the trade's supply chain. The problem here is distributors honoring arcane and vestigial agreements penned with Amazon in the 90's that do not make sense in today's market.

The intended role a distributor provides is to connect a publisher's catalog of forthcoming works (a **Frontlist**) to a network of booksellers. Distributors are also meant to be curatorial tastemakers, selecting the publishers they represent with integrity equal to a publisher making their choices on who to publish. This creates wholesale relationships between publishers and booksellers, and forges authorities in publishers who stand up talent both fledgling and established. These distributors service Amazon in addition to other big-box retail and e-commerce giants.

The issue at hand is that purchaser behaviors have largely migrated to online retailers—Amazon as an obvious default—while brick-and-mortar independent retailers reduce in size and meaningful sales volume, some publishers see Amazon taking up a majority share of their distributor sales.

The original function of the distributor creating bonds between publisher and bookseller seems drastically diluted as the priority shifts to filling larger Amazon orders. This often leaves distributors appearing more like a superfluous *pass-through entity* for passionless purchases online; taking a cut on a sales channel that require no human intervention, typically stirred up via the distribution capital of the publisher or author to begin with.

New types of distribution models are emerging today that do not require exclusivity over a represented publisher's catalog, meaning the publisher can open up their own accounts with Amazon and fill orders directly through programs such as **Amazon Advantage** or **Amazon Seller Central** (Fulfilled by Amazon or FBA) or **Kindle Direct Publishing** (KDP). Both the margins and cashflow potential in this direct control of e-commerce accounts are becoming increasingly crucial for smaller/start-up publishers to consider as they enter the market. Even mid-to-large sized publishers can use their weight to strike non-exclusivity deals with distributors, carving out digital rights or even the entire Amazon account.

PROBLEMS WITH PRINTERS

We can thank the 90s through the aughts for the domestic manufacturing drought we are in today. We saw massive supply chain disruptions in 2020's pandemic era that resulted in book paper shortages that lasted through 2023. It feels back to normal now here in 2024, although book paper and printing costs have generally *doubled* across the board since 2020.

Offset Printing remains the way to go for large-volume printing. There are a handful of competitive options in the United States, although it's easy to outsource to China for high quality large-run book manufacturing that is ridiculously cheap. However, today's tariffs on China (which get passed onto us, the business, and then you, the reader) make this option not as marginally beneficial as it used to be.

As I've cudgeled into your head by now, print on demand *is* and *is still becoming* increasingly pervasive. This author believes it will be the primary default of book manufacturing a decade from now.

PROBLEMS AUTHORS FACE

If you're new talent that does not have some sort of platform, some kind of parasocial relationship with your audience that gives you ridiculous distribution capital, it's hard to find a publisher or representation that will give you the time of day. This doesn't exactly mean you need a big social media following. Of course it helps, it's a solid tool. There are ways to manufacture a platform beyond social media, but social media is a risk-mitigating factor in today's venture capital mindset of book publishing.

Literary agents are increasingly difficult to find as advances are inconsistent—again, an impact of risk aversion. As such, there are very few independent literary agents, and literary representation is now largely dominated by Creative Artists Agency (CAA) and William Morris Endeavor (WME), where they can take their brand name talent and funnel their works to the bigger publishers.

There are still, of course, independent publishers and agents of integrity that can spot and build new talent. The players are few and far between, and they all participate in the vibes roulette of our business. This speaks to the VC mindset; a confluence of taste, integrity, and grit—seeing the future in the face of unknown odds. But like any good strategic partner, it's hard to find in today's landscape, and sometimes doing it yourself is better than doing it half-assed with a publisher who has no skin in the game.

PROBLEMS WITH SMALL PUBLISHING / START-UP PUBLISHING:

"What good is a publisher?" asks the high distribution capital individual. "If you're relying on me and my network to shill my book, what good are you?"

Great question. Big publishers solve for this by paying fat advances and offering legacy brand authority. Smaller publishers have to compete hard in order to prove value over what high distribution individuals can achieve themselves with today's highly robust self-publishing tools.

Smaller publishers can compete by scaling up to the same levels of distribution as the Big Five, or using Big Five distributors, or creating their own distribution that services these accounts. At the end of the day, distribution is a plateau; there are only so many sales channels and reps behind them in addition to their heavy skew toward Amazon sales.

This leaves new or smaller publishers in a position to get creative with their offerings, how they market them, and how they choose to make them available. A big example of a simple blind spot in bigger publishers are *cool events*. It's uncommon to see publishers offer their authorship a book tour or even a *single event*. Generally authors, especially new talent, are left to their own devices to figure out the events surrounding their book release; they often are responsible for doing it themselves or finding third party promoter support.

While capital intensive, there are ways of standing up tours that can have a reasonable target of breaking even with a solid ticketing model. The quality of marketing from sublime in-person experiences translates very well into lasting word-of-mouth awareness campaigns, and are good content pipelines in and of themselves if you record your programs. I can't stress this enough; curating a space where an audience can have a good time is probably one of the most valuable things on the planet Earth.

A final problem small publishers face is the private equity-ization of everything; consolidations across distribution, printing, and publishing. While publishers on a micro level (a title by title basis) have to think like venture capitalists, publishers on a macro level have to think like private equity. Because most of it is owned by private equity. Simon & Schuster this last fall was sold to top PE firm KKR.

What this means is that the incentive is to keep a mature asset improving on an annual basis. This compounds the issue of risk assessment and value association in book publishing, creating constraints around acquisition choices that simply did not exist thirty years ago.

In total, this amalgam of problems has created a large, flat, stagnant surface with a massive saturation of content. This poses a challenging playing field for emerging authors and publishers alike. However, this has also created new opportunities for disruption and competitiveness against extremely boring and hegemonic publishers, crafting entirely original paths for success.

II

A PUBLISHER TODAY

The core function of book publishing can be reduced into two high-level roles; editorial (managing editor or editor-in-chief) and production (production director). Editorial remains the same since the days of Guttenburg; a publisher selects a work, purchases a license to be the sole publisher of the work for a term, edits a manuscript into a book (acting as a bridge between author and reader), designs that book into a sleek product, and distributes the finished book to readers throughout the world. What has changed largely rests in the means of production and distribution, influencing how editorial starts to begin with.

We are living in a glorious time of unprecedented content democratization across all cultural industries. Enterprise tools that were otherwise price-gated, infrastructures of distribution that were once capital and logistically intensive, have since been digitized and packaged for the individual consumer—or independent creator. This trend has replicated itself across multiple industries in the exact way Marc Andreessen stated in his 2011 essay "Why Software Is Eating The World."

> "Six decades into the computer revolution, four decades since the invention of the microprocessor, and two decades into the rise of the modern Internet, all of the technology required to transform industries through software finally works and can be widely delivered at global scale."
>
> — Marc Andreessen,
> "Why Software Is Eating The World"

In the case of book publishing, the software of eBooks and eCommerce signaled a massive disruption in how publishers get their content in the hands of readers. What emerged is a form of digitization that has and continues to cause an indelible transformation not just in how books are purchased but *how they are published*—print on demand. Consider the amount of books **Bowker** reported being published in 2010; approximately 328,259 books between traditional and self-published titles. In 2010 there were 2,600 active book publishers in the United States according to the Association of American Publishers. In 2023, Bowker reported approximately four million titles, but still only around 2,700 active book publishers in the United States

These numbers express the sheer scale of content saturation accelerated by the growth of print-on-demand tools such as **Ingram's LightningSource** (LSI) and **Amazon's Kindle Direct Publishing** (KDP) program. These tools offer not just swift, automated book production but also include a new style of distribution to the book trade, enabling the individual self-publisher to blast their digital title across a vast net of sales channels—Amazon, Barnes & Noble, **Ingram's iPage**, Bookshop.org—sales channels that now command a dominating eCommerce presence.

It used to be the case that these sales channels only existed in brick-and-mortar environments, but with Amazon's early monopoly on eCommerce, it forced big-box retail giants such as Target, Walmart, and Barnes & Noble to create their own platforms in the digital marketplace. This also spurred on the development of Bookshop.org, which is backed by Ingram and Koch money with Ingram serving as their exclusive source of fulfillment. I unpack the nuances of **Ingram Industries** throughout this book and in the chapter "A Tangent Down the Ingram Rabbit Hole."

One of the most famous casualties of this seemingly overnight shift from brick-and-mortar to eCommerce dominion was the collapse of Borders Booksellers, which had a cascading ripple effect throughout the industry. One of the primary reasons Borders folded was because it outsourced its eCommerce sales exclusively to Amazon, using them to warehouse and fill orders. Instead of investing in their own online sales solutions (something that would have been quite competitive given their retail and distribution capabilities), they expanded their physical locations, becoming over-extended in long term leases while earning sub-optimal margins on online sales. As reader purchases trended more online, they imploded under their own weight in 2011.

Book purchasing decisions, both in a wholesale sense (appealing to bookseller representatives that make large acquisitions for retail) and a retail sense (the reader) have only continued to trend online. The two leading wholesale portals that exist to acquire books are **Ingram's iPage** and **Edelweiss+**. Between these platforms and the purchase behaviors of readers on Amazon, more than 80% of a book's exposure now happens online.

This is a compelling dynamic to consider as we think about the distribution channels offered to the print-on-demand object, to the self-publisher, what it means for the future of publishing at large, and what it means when starting up a new publishing property.

Distribution to booksellers and libraries (also known as distribution to the book trade or **trade distribution**) requires a publisher to overcome hedges of scale; in order to be seriously considered as a client to a trade distributor, a publisher needs to have an established **backlist** that's generating at least X amount of topline revenue from wholesales (the X fluctuates depending on the size of distributor; smaller distributors generally require ~100K topline, while larger ones require 2MM) in addition to a committed annual **frontlist** output (some smaller distributors are content with no frontlist commitment, others require at least 2-6 titles a year, while bigger distributors expect anywhere between 8-20 titles a year).

This creates a hedge of volume to overcome when just starting out. The fledgling publisher has a fork ahead of them: distribute to the trade using the print-on-demand grid or don't distribute to the trade when starting out. While there are pitfalls in the POD grid, it's likely a better path to explore in lieu of ignoring building up your backlist with exposure to the trade via these exclusively digital corridors. Combining these tools in tandem with a direct sales channel (an eCommerce website of your own, fulfilling your own titles from your apartment or a dingy windowless storage unit like I used to) gives your titles some degree of exposure while also affording the start-up publisher the agility to not be bogged down by inventory, storage, and other various warehouse logistics.

It is perhaps reductive to say there's simply a fork ahead of the fledgling publisher. There are a myriad of other things that could occur to provide avenues of opportunity, such as aggregating publishing projects with your colleagues to achieve volume, or spending your life savings to accelerate acquisitions to build up a massive frontlist, or even opening up accounts with each disparate sales channel and being your own distributor; there are innovative solutions to these problems, I'm sure of it!

The point is, trade distribution and a diversification of where your titles are placed is necessary in capturing the most retail value possible for your product, as well as providing the most value to your author. Let us not forget, we as publishers owe it to our authors to give their titles the most access and exposure possible—distribution to the trade is the only way your titles cross the radar of libraries, educators, and independent booksellers. Furthermore, the reality is, most readers are content to default to the ease of Amazon. If you can build value by circumventing these channels by building your own distribution infrastructure, such as Powell's booksellers did back in 2019, all the more power to you.

CURATION

One must consider, well, if a start-up publisher would utilize the same tools that are accessible to the self-publishing author, why do I even need a publisher? This begs the question, what does a publisher even do?

The responsibility at its core, beyond the administration, capitalization, and productization layers on top of it, is curation. It is discerning a list of quality letters that speaks to something. Something can be a scene, a moment in time that influences the culture, eventually moving downstream *becoming* the culture. It can be a movement. It can be a certain cluster of intellectuals, it can be a specific genre authority, it can be a joke everyone is in on. As prolific author L. Ron Hubbard discovered, it could be a religion. The thematic thrust is mercurial and vibey; this is, perhaps, why it is so difficult to orchestrate and sustain. It is something not so much seen but felt. The publisher captures and curates the vibe; it is nothing less than catching lightning in a bottle.

That electricity could resonate for decades or die out within a year; and indeed some frontlists behave this way. Some publishers such as Regnery saw phenomenal frontlist performance accounting for 90% of their annual topline, but year after year only saw their astronomical backlist of over 5,000 titles account for a nominal 10% of their annual revenues. What that speaks to is the viral (flash in the pan) quality of their titles versus the perennial (timeless) quality of their titles.

Striking bestseller status is what earns a publisher pips on their collar; a sharpshooter publisher with a bestselling trend of acquisitions will be said to have a "golden gun." But a publisher that achieves not just bestselling status, but perennial status, hits a nerve that goes far deeper than a viral sensation. It is a mercurial and profound art enabling authors and editors to create timeless works, and there is no way for me to explain how that happens beyond the boots on the ground vibe-sifting that publishers must build their lives around.

This is the question I pose to the budding publisher looking to start out; what is it you hope to speak to? It is not dissimilar to the questions authors must ask themselves when setting out to write and publish a book. This is a symbiotic relationship, with a symbiotic goal of reach and timelessness. This is inevitably colored by the economic reality we live inside of, one of competition and growth. As such we come full circle to the hedge of volume demanded by distribution to the trade; and here we see more clearly the additional layers of responsibility taken on by the publisher.

A book's production, discerning how a book is made—the volume of the print run, the type of paper, the finishing of the cover to give it that extra oomph—informs who is assigned to design the book. This task is a union of the curatorial vibe of aesthetics and productization, a visual and physical encapsulation of the core task of vibemaking. Determining vendors, print costs, and volume is a task of product management and risk assessment.

This decision-making happens in tandem with the scope of distribution. If you want to print ten thousand units of a book, how will it reach readers and booksellers? How are booksellers even communicated with?

This is the gate kept by publishers with traditional distribution to the trade. A distributor completes the logistical function of storing and sending books at wholesale volume, but also distributors of scale stage sales conferences generally three times a year. These are in-person functions where sales representatives responsible for acquisitions and awareness of any given title meet and discuss frontlists. This is where a publisher makes their presence known, their curatorial vibe codified in the minds of those who ultimately distribute such discerning taste.

There exists a new wave of distributors to the book trade that do not require such lofty volume to provide basic services and also do not require exclusivity from the publishers they represent, leaning into some of the new systems of digital distribution that we've outlined so far. Examples of these distributors are Small Press Distributors in Berkeley and Asterism Books in Seattle. Both of these distributors offer a good starting point to allow publishers to scale their lists but do not offer larger awareness or logistical engines that the top layer of distributors sport (details that will be outlined in the chapter "Comparison of Legacy & New Models").

Between editorial and production, we see how these core decisions trickle down through the rest of the book publishing chain, informing catalog (the list of books coming out from a publisher any given season), distribution (how this catalog makes it to readers), and print (how the book is manufactured).

CATALOG

This isn't a book about *what* to publish. It's my hope that your publishing journey is a natural extension of your life's journey, but how you play this game is up to you. What I will speak to here is the productization of a manuscript into a book, and when we color in the element of distribution, the pacing of a publisher's seasonal releases.

A publisher's catalog is the combined works of their **imprint**. An imprint is simply another name for a publishing house, like a record label or a sub label. Some publishers are multiple imprints combined, also known as a **publishing group**. Imprints are generally broken out from their larger publishing group to define a specific project or genre category they wish to speak to. An example of this is Penguin Classics, an imprint of Penguin Random House. Penguin Classics specifically focuses on titles in the public domain that Penguin has some degree of rights participation with; these are books they find to be important (or money makers) in the perennial, classical sense.

A **frontlist** are titles that are forthcoming. Sometimes what defines a frontlist can change depending on what kind of sales channel or distributor you are talking to. I define a title as having frontlist status for a full year from its publishing date, others will say frontlist status ends as soon as the season in which it was published does. This is mildly subjective.

A **publishing date** is a day, typically set on a Tuesday, where a title becomes available anywhere books are sold. This is also known as its on-sale date. This edition of *A Book About Books* has a publishing date set to March 11, 2025. This means that I will have a presale campaign leading up to November 19, 2024, and upon that date this book will be in the hands of readers who have ordered it online (or will, at least, be on the way to them), and will appear on the shelves of booksellers who have chosen to acquire it.

Tuesdays are a typical default for publishing dates because these are the days where booksellers restock their inventory, and distributors have dispatched new orders; a natural rhythm of logistics. Tuesday is also the day of Mars, the God of War. A good day to tackle large to-do items, handle more laborious tasks, and stage integral meetings. Read into that however you see fit.

Some distributors work on a three-calendar season; but I prefer a two-calendar season, so I will be depicting examples of a two-calendar season throughout this book. Learning a three-calendar season is not too much of a logical leap from a two-calendar schedule.

Using a two-calendar schedule, a frontlist is defined in a Spring/Summer or Fall/Winter season. With ABAB's publishing date of March 4, 2025, it is frontlist for the Spring/Summer 2025 season. We will unfold this calendar groove in the distribution section.

A **backlist** is everything that has come out. This is a publisher's greatest asset; titles that have been paid for, printed, marketed, released, and delivered to the hands of readers. It is the responsibility of the publisher to steward their backlist, to continue making their titles accessible to the readership, and for the more cunning—to exploit the myriad of profit corridors that exist with the bedrock IP that are books. More on that in the "Intellectual Property & Rights" section.

Backlist titles generally arrive at a fork in their lifespans; reaching some degree of perennial status or drifting into obscurity and ultimately reaching out-of-print status (although there is no reason for anything to go out of print any longer, which I will expand upon in the "Printing" chapter of this section).

Each year, a publisher, informed by the deadlines put forward by their distributor on their seasonal calendars, acquires titles and develops them into books. It is generally good form for a publisher to issue a letter of intent to soft-acquire a title for development before producing a publishing contract after a manuscript has reached a certain stage of maturity. There are an array of states a manuscript takes in its raw form; the scope of when a manuscript is ready to be a book could be small or huge—there's no way to fully articulate all of the variables that can inform the scope of this task. It comes down to editorial sense, and how heavy of a hand a publisher wants to lay down in order to craft the raw material into its final form.

Here we arrive at the great art of bookmaking: the editorial process. This constitutes editing, proofreading, and design. There are entire books written about editing, proofreading, and design, so I will not endeavor to write another. But I will speak to the spirit of these categories; the best publishers I know are truly discerning editors in how they not only select the works they wish to publish, but how they best position an author's writing to the reading public. This is done through the often painful, hopefully generative, process of editing.

This requires a sublime degree of trust between the editor and author. Some authors are like wild mares blazing the fields, gallantly thrusting their majesty for all to behold. Such beasts do not like to be broken in and made easy for casual riders. Others are a little more agreeable when it comes to a capable jockey. Trust and a type of symbiotic mind-meld is a hard thing to come by, but when it does, it produces a stunning gem from an otherwise unpolished stone.

Remember, a quality editor is thinking about the reader, not the writer.

Proofreading is obvious and I will not expand upon it. It is mundane, but the most important things in life live exuberantly in the mundane. I will bet a dollar that this process will someday soon be completely automated by some nifty AI tool. In fact, I used Chat GPT-4o to proofread this book. Write to me if it missed anything.

Design! In addition to making compelling acquisitions, this is where a publisher can truly set themselves apart from the static and noise of an ever scaling volume of annually published titles. It astonishes me that some publishers get away with producing the most on-rails undergraduate photoshop class looking book jackets one has ever encountered. This is yet another evasive subjective space where I cannot offer more than, *make it good*, make it timeless. What is that? *Indeed*. Explore, study, emulate but do not copy.

The thing about book design is that it is heavily informed by the book's desired print parameters. The type of paper used, the finishing specifications, whether it's **casebound** or **perfect bound**; these are but a few of the variables that inform how a book is designed. More on this in the "Printing" chapter of this section. A good book designer that sets themselves beyond other book designers has a command of how printing and binding mechanically works; they understand the end product.

A publisher, particularly one starting out, is commanding each of these categories of what makes a book. Everything from the initial vibe impulse on an acquisition to its development from manuscript into a book is an extension of the publisher's sensibilities, creating not just readable content of perennial quality, but an object that expresses the exact same degree of timelessness. These efforts work together to produce a sublime reading experience, a catalog that stands for eternity.

DISTRIBUTION

We have been enjoying a stroll through a neatly manicured lawn contemplating the art of curating a catalog and have now arrived at a massive hedge. On the other side of this hedge is the palatial estate that is the book trade. Gosh, are they having a party? They are. They are all having a party without you, talking about the publishers they like, the awards they'll deliver to a select handful of frontlist titles, the priority shelf space they'll allot catalogs they appreciate from publishers they like and trust.

This isn't *Eyes Wide Shut*; a password isn't going to cut it. How are we getting in?

Distributors assess three things when considering a new client to on-board: the content of the catalog and how it fits in with their overall milieu, the topline revenue earned from wholesales by a publisher's catalog on an annual basis, and the frontlist output a publisher will commit themselves to moving forward.

Distributors come in a few shapes and sizes, but they all serve a singular entity: the book trade. The book trade is everyone and everything involved in the distribution and sale of books. It is a union of sales channels and distributors. Publishers feed the book trade with their catalogs, and make appeals to the trade to pitch the relevance of their work to a broader readership that they provide access to.

Distributors service sales channels with inventory at discounted wholesale rates. Sales channels include booksellers, libraries, educators, and wholesalers of books. They are, but are not limited to:

Big Retail / Big eCommerce
    Amazon
    Barnes & Noble
    Target, Walmart, Costco (I relegate these to

a singular line because they are only in the business of a particular type of mass-market paperback, and aren't necessarily *booksellers*, even though they sell books.)

Bookshop.org

Wholesalers

Ingram; visit page 83 for the chapter I have dedicated to Ingram Industries. Take note now, Ingram is a massive force in the global book trade that constitutes many verticles of business including print and distribution. They are the largest wholesaler of books on the planet Earth. A vast majority of the book trade (80% give or take) use Ingram's online web tool iPage to browse catalogs and make wholesale acquisitions.

Baker & Taylor; this wholesaler primarily services American libraries. Libraries can make acquisitions via Ingram, but generally do it through regional board acquisitions that occur through Baker & Taylor.

Independent Booksellers

There are still some 500 competitive indie booksellers in the United States as of 2024. Independent booksellers either make acquisitions direct through Ingram, or direct from distributors. There are a myriad of regional bookseller associations as well as national bookseller associations that help inform independent bookseller choices. But this is where the art of being an independent bookseller still thrives— this is where an individual can still make compelling, out-of-the-box choices.

Universities / Education

Certain titles can get adopted into a school's curriculum. Great for a title as this creates consistent & required wholesale purchases. Universities will make acquisitions either from the distributor or via a wholesaler (**Ingram**) to fulfill their university bookstore.

International Wholesalers; we're focusing on the English-speaking market

PGC/Raincoast fulfills the Canadian bookseller market

IPS UK fulfills the United Kingdom & EU markets

Newsouth fulfills Australian markets

An easy point to conflate here is the difference between a wholesaler and a distributor. A simple differentiator that I lifted from the publisher Janaka Stucky is that a distributor is an *active* sales force while a wholesaler is a *passive* sales force. A distributor actively represents a publisher's catalog, generating an awareness campaign to the trade, while a wholesaler simply makes the inventory accessible for acquisition. A distributor will make a title available to a wholesaler at a discounted rate, and the wholesaler will again re-sell it for a slightly marked up rate, making a thin margin but at volume.

Why not just purchase from a distributor instead of a wholesaler? Well, you can. The thing is, wholesalers like Ingram make it convenient for purchasers by aggregating everything in one place across distributors, and providing discounts for volume. Otherwise, you would have to make an account with every disparate distributor that represents disparate catalogs.

There are three categories of book distributor—big, specialized, and small. The big distributors all compete at a fairly similar level and represent publishers that would consider the other their contemporaries.

The Big Five book publishers—Penguin Random House (owned by the German media conglomerate Bertelsmann), MacMillan, Harper Collins (owned by Rupert Murdoch's News Corp), Hachette, and Simon & Schuster (freshly acquired by private equity firm KKR in a sale from Paramount Global) —each have their own distribution corps vertically integrated under their umbrella of operations. An independent publisher can be distributed to the trade by Simon & Schuster, have their catalog represented to the trade by Simon & Schuster, use Simon & Schuster's warehousing and fulfillment logistics to fulfill wholesale orders across sales channels, but not be a Simon & Schuster imprint owned by Simon & Schuster. See the section "Comparison of Legacy & New Models" for more on this.

The other big distributor is now Ingram. Yes, *that* Ingram, the world's largest wholesaler of books. In 2016 they went on an acquisitions frenzy, deciding that it was time for them to also actively represent publishers and, yes, sell wholesale inventory to themselves so that they could resell their own inventory at a slightly higher wholesale rate. The distributors that they acquired were Publishers Group West, Perseus Book Group, Two Rivers, and Consortium. In one fell swoop they acquired the representation of over 1,000 publisher catalogs, and created an entirely new distribution environment competitive with the Big Five—Ingram Content Group.

The distributors of the Big Five and ICG each have their ups and downs depending on what you value as a publisher. An example of upside with being distributed by PRH is their sheer volume; they represent over a thousand publishers, and as such can offer competitively smaller rates for their services. Additionally, PRH owns their own offset and digital printers, and can offer inventory solutions for their publishers. However, scale can work against you; every two account representatives at PRH is handling ~150 publishers. The amount of bespoke sales and marketing attention gets lost, and priorities are placed on bigger fish or longer-standing relationships.

Consortium on the other hand has a seasoned league of 35 account representatives and only represents 150 publishers. It could be argued that Consortium has a much more hands-on understanding of the catalogs they represent; however, their fees are decently higher.

Let's take a look at how this mutual economy functions. For this example we will consider the book of poetry *Notes on Shapeshifting* by Gabi Abrāo, published by Not a Cult, distributed to the trade by Consortium.

Notes on Shapeshifting has a list price of $18.95. A list price is another word for retail price, the price a reader pays at a bookstore

The distributor makes this title available at a wholesale rate of $9.48. Half of the title's list price. The distributor takes 26% of the wholesale price; their fee in this case is $2.47. The publisher is left with a net compensation of $7.01, less other fees that operate in the background such as storage and freight fees that nickel and dime the publisher in an aggregate sum based on volume on a monthly basis.

Let's circle back to consider how a wholesaler makes their money when purchasing from a distributor to resell their inventory to booksellers. Wholesalers like Ingram (via iPage) typically sell their available titles for 30% - 40% off the title's list price to booksellers, depending on the combined volume the bookseller makes acquisitions at. It's within that 10% - 20% margin the wholesaler makes their net profit.

A 26% cut by Consortium is relatively high, but is generally the starting default. This distributor's fee scales down depending on the combined topline revenue from the publisher. This is the main negotiating vehicle a publisher has when entertaining distribution options to the trade; the combined backlist and topline annual earnings. An example of this is Skyhorse Publishing; with over 10,000 titles in their backlist with a combined 450-500 titles produced annually in their frontlist, Skyhorse's distributor Simon & Schuster only takes 6% from their wholesales. The incentive of volume!

So, wait. Couldn't I, a fledgling publisher, simply open an account with Ingram to sell my catalog directly to them and earn 60% - 70% of my list price while still making it available on the largest wholesale channel in the world? Yes, of course. Presumably, representation by a distributor is adding a layer of value on your catalog that otherwise wouldn't be there. What is this value?

This value is largely driven by the inside-industry awareness campaign directed toward the book trade through the form of a sales conference. Each distributor has their own sales conference for each calendar season; a Spring/Summer sales conference and a Fall/Winter sales conference. There are additional sales conferences that happen independently of distributors held by bookseller associations, such as the Winter Institute, as well as more regional sales conferences. With the democratization of distribution and the propagation of published titles, this remains a primary method to inject content into the artery of the mainstream.

The sales conference has two stages that take place before the actual conference: title on-boarding and the presales meeting. Title on-boarding takes place one year in advance of the publishing season. This is where a publisher declares the titles they intend to publish and distribute to the trade. Distributors each have some kind of internal database that manages the on-boarding of titles and houses all of a book's metadata. In the case of the Ingram properties, this tool is called CoreSource. Simon & Schuster has Portal. PRH has MyHouse. And so on.

The distribution team has a one-on-one meeting with their publisher client, and provides them with their first bout of feedback on draft one of their title listings. The publisher processes these notes in preparation for the presales conference; a dry run of the sales conference. This is where the title starts to list out to wholesale channels such as Edelweiss+ and Ingram's iPage. Generally during a meeting like this, Edelweiss+ is open and the distribution team is scrutinizing the listing for best practices. Feedback is issued in advance of the sales conference.

The sales conference typically happens in person, though an increasingly online or "hybrid" approach has been unfolding since 2020. This is where the publisher gets on a stage and makes their frontlist presentation to the trade, revealing their forthcoming titles and making a case for why this title is something they, the trade, should be interested in and put their efforts behind. A part of this presentation is all of the promotional efforts that will be put behind the title—this author will tour to X cities during X dates, has appearances scheduled on X podcasts, will have reviews on X publications— and essentially encourages the trade that this title is going to be a hit should they make the choice to acquire the title and shelve it simultaneously, rallying around the publishing date and hitting the release with coordinated force.

Everyone in this coordinated effort wins if a title hits bestseller status during the week of its release, and hopefully beyond. The social network of the book trade is fundamental to the success of books, and is what makes a trade distribution partnership worth its cut of margin. While there is immense value in the presentation component of the sales conference, I would say the vast majority of the value is in everything around the conference.

Dozens of reps all consolidated in one city for a few days. Consider the dinners, the conversations over drinks, the discussions between presentations; the clubhouse of it all. It is the party beyond the hedge. This is where a publisher and the vibe they curate gets known. Put enough time and reps into this process, in this relatively small pool of people, and not just a singular title gets elevated—but the entire catalog by way of reputation. This is, most importantly, how new talent gets evangelized.

* * *

Without volume—publishers just starting in standing up their lists, or publishers who for whatever reason don't make significant topline revenue from wholesales—the fledgling publisher turns to the smaller distributors. The primary example of this is in the namesake; Small Press Distributors. SPD does not have the same requirements as the big distributors, providing a far more accessible approach to the trade than the bigger distributors. However, they do not have a sales conference, leaving engine-building of an awareness campaign solely to the publisher.

The upside here is that it removes a step in having to create an account with every disparate sales channel, resulting in a convenient centralized node to interact with for wholesales, providing the publisher with an easier environment for scale. The new Asterism Books – one of the first new distributors to emerge in the last decade or two – provides a similar level of service.

Or—OR!—a start-up publisher can cut out third parties entirely. Here is where we land back at my emphasis on the interesting technology of print on demand. Remember, Ingram is the largest wholesaler of books and now also contains a league of distributors competitive to the Big Five. In addition to this, Ingram is the global leader in print on demand.

"Why in the world are we wallpapering the warehouse with books? Wouldn't it be better to store a digital file and print a book when there was demand?"

— John Ingram, surviving heir and current chairman of Ingram Industries

LightningSource was started by Ingram back in 1997 at the edge of the dot-com era. At the end of 1998, LightningSource had 1,500 titles in their library. Today, over 4,000 titles get uploaded to LightningSource a day. There's nothing stopping you from adding to this figure.

PRINTING

There are two ways to print a book intended for trade release; digital printing or offset printing. Offset printing is a high-quality cost-effective method of printing that has been around for centuries. On the most basic level, it involves transferring ink from a metal plate to a rubber blanket and then onto paper. The technical details are best explained by this neat 1.5 minute video embedded in this QR code.

Because of the laborious setup requirements for off-set printing, it is only used for jobs of volume—the long run. Some offset printers will take a job with as few as 500 units, but typically the minimum is at 1,000 units. You generally see price breaks on a per unit basis every 500 to 1,000 units printed.

For jobs under 500 units, the short run, we deploy digital printing. Digital printing is a relatively new innovation using toner to quickly turn around digital files into print format. While there is no extensive setup in digital printing, the cost of toner and the licensing model behind commercial digital printers make it so that there are no price breaks; it costs as much to print a single book as it does to print 500. The licensing model behind commercial digital printers is what's known as a "cost per click."

When you purchase a commercial digital printer from, say, Xerox or HP; you purchase a service contract with the printer. The service contract entitles you to 24/7 support from the vendor if anything goes awry with the printer, and the vendor refills the toner when it depletes. But the vendor continues to extract revenue from the printer every time it is used. Software that manages the printer keeps the vendor informed of every time a sheet is fed through the printer, and keeps score of the toner deployed per job, charging the printer a "cost per click"—costs passed on to the client using the printer's service. This is why digital printing, while sometimes not even as good of quality as offset printing, is comparatively expensive per unit.

Printing is a third of the job of manufacturing a book. Another third is binding. **Perfect binding** is typically used for mass-distributed paperbacks (known as **trade paperbacks**). It is called "perfect binding" because the glue sets in such a way that is intended to be nearly invisible; *perfect*. Today's glue technology is known as PUR glue—polyurethane. Polyurethane is among the most advanced of glue technology and is used in perfect binding books to give it the most archival life; perfect binding using PUR is supposed to last well over one hundred years.

The final third is finishing. Finishing is twofold; utility and aesthetic. For a paperback, the utility is the cover's coating. The two main categories of coating are gloss or matte. Both incorporate a UV protectant to resist sun damage and are semi water-resistant. The coating seals in the cover's paper, giving it decades of durability over uncoated stocks. The aesthetic possibilities are manifold; foiling, spot varnishes, debossing, and embossing are a handful of ways to provide added flair to a book's look.

The world of casebound printing—also known as

hardcover books—is vast. There are many ways to produce a casebound book, from scalable trade releases to very fancy short run releases. The interior printing of a casebound book behaves much the same as a paperback, save for one crucial difference in the binding. While you can perfect-bind a casebound book's interior book block, a more traditional and archival way of binding a casebound book is by smyth-sewing the book.

Smyth-sewn book binding is a durable method where folded signatures are stitched together with thread, then glued to the spine, allowing books to lay flat when open. Here is a good video explanation on smyth-sewing:

What makes a *hardcover* cover *hard* is the chip board. The chip board, like paper, has varying weights and qualities—it's basically a piece of dense cardboard—that then has material wrapped around it and glued to its interior, the folds of which are glued beneath the endpapers at either end of the book. There are a huge variety of materials that can be used to wrap around a chip board; heavy coated paper, different cloths, leathers, and so on.

Book printers taking jobs for books to be distributed by the trade have to be scalable. As such, each third of this process—printing, binding, and finishing—are done in-line; meaning the vendor handles each aspect of the process in-house without having to outsource any part of the job. There still exist disparate printers, binderies, and finishers for very particular jobs. But to scale, you must find either a digital or offset printer that can produce books end-to-end in-line.

Looking at our example with *Notes on Shapeshifting*, here is a quote from the offset printer Marquis—one of the most competitive in-line offset printers servicing the book trade on the North American continent.

NOT A CULT, LLC

To the attention of: *DANIEL LISI/CO OWNER*

We are pleased to present our prices and conditions for the following job quoted in accordance with your specifications.

TITLE	NOTES ON SHAPEHIFTING
TRIM SIZE :	5.5 X 8.5
NUMBER OF PAGES:	96
INSIDE INK:	1(BLACK) / 1(BLACK), WITHOUT BLEEDS
INK COVERAGE:	
INSIDE PAPER:	55 LB ENVIRO BOOK NATURAL 81 GSM (FSC-100) - 420 P
COVER PRINTING :	4(PROCESS) / 0
COVER FINISHING :	MATTE LAMINATION
MATERIAL:	10PTS C1C (FSC-MIX)
BINDING:	SPLIT PB AND HC
MATERIAL SUPPLIED (INSIDE):	FINAL FILE + REMOTE PROOF
MATERIAL SUPPLIED (COVER):	FINAL FILE + REMOTE PROOF
EPUB FILE :	NOT INCLUDED
OVER-RUNS AND UNDER-RUNS	TOLERANCE OF 10%
OTHER:	

QTY:	6,500
PAGES:	96
UNIT :	$1.9630
TOTAL:	$12,759.50
ADD'L:	$1.7670
SPINE:	2.566"
WEIGHT:	3081 LBS
DELIVERY:	FOB PLANT
TERMS:	NET 60
NOTES:	PRICE VALID FOR IMMEDIATE PRODUCTION
	1500 CASEBIND (2 VERSION OF CASE WRAP) + 5000 PERFECT BIND BOOK
	100LB 4/0 ON 100LB TEXT + MATTE LAM + STAMP ON FRONT & SPINE OVER 90PT BOARD ROUND B/
	ENDPAPER ON 80LB OFFSET CREAM UNPRINTED. MATCHING H&T BAND

Here we see that the per-unit cost of a 6,500-unit order is (rounding up) $1.97. Let's consider our back of the napkin math of the distributor take on this title from before; the wholesale price of *Notes on Shapeshifting* is $9.48, the distributor's 26% fee is $2.47, and our net from this exchange is $7.01. Knowing the wholesale pricing and fees is how we determine a target for our printing cost, and what we can safely price the book at; $18.95. Our actual net receipt on *Notes on Shapeshifting* less the printing cost is $5.04.

When determining a retail price for a book, we have to consider if our margin on maximal wholesale discounts is "safe." I generally look for at least two times the return on a wholesale versus the print cost.

We can shave off cost on this print job by cutting off embellishments such as the foil stamping on the cover and spine; we could use slightly thinner paper, a 50lb stock in lieu of a 55lb stock. With these decisions, we see how the book's design is ultimately influenced by how the book is being printed; manufacturing and design are considered in tandem, and are ultimately informed by the economics of making a title available to the trade.

PRINT ON DEMAND

Print on demand uses digital printers to print book blocks. Services like IngramSpark and Amazon's Kindle Direct Publishing program use software and an automated in-line manufacturing process to print, coat their covers, and perfect bind their books without any human touch. Both services have print grids on six continents, so if a customer purchases a book in Australia, the book is automatically manufactured in Australia and shipped regionally, and so on.

What makes a service like IngramSpark even more compelling is that the service has an option to "enable distribution," which makes the title available across nearly all of the sales channels detailed in the Distribution section as an eCommerce object available for retail or wholesale. Imagine that. From the comfort of your own home, by yourself, you can blast a title out across the world using IngramSpark and KDP in tandem, capturing all sales channels digitally.

The book you're holding now deploys this method. If you flip to the very last page of this book, you will find a CPSIA QR code; this is the maker's mark of all print-on-demand objects. I deployed this title in this way to serve as an example of the comparable distribution reach of the digital print-on-demand grid. The future of book publishing will continue to trend in this direction; publishers will digitize their sprawling backlists, storing their titles in the cloud rather than overstocking warehouses. Right now it's still competitive to produce an upfront offset printing, but as POD becomes more sophisticated, we may see a day where books are exclusively produced using these digitized systems.

There are downsides to print on demand. For starters, the range of options for manufacturing are on-rails. The paper types and finishing options are limited; POD is not presently capable of producing the elegant foil stamping found on *Notes on Shapeshifting*. Smyth sewing is presently not an option, only perfect binding.

Quality assurance is the biggest pitfall – there are a lot of things that can go wrong in a purely automated system. Trimming can be coarse, color fidelity can be less than desirable, accuracy on spine alignment can be off. Sometimes print-on-demand systems skip a beat in their line and an entirely incorrect book interior could be placed inside of the wrong jacket! There is no human touch, unlike the quality assurance found in craft digital printers and offset printers that assure precision and beauty behind the craft.

This speaks overall to the greatest downside of automated digital systems; the missing human element. This is true as well in the digital distribution side of things. If the self-publisher decides to take this route and purely digitize their distribution using print-on-demand, you also cut out the human awareness campaign of the book trade. With no distributors, sales conferences, or hob-nobbing with reps, how does a book penetrate its way into the minds of booksellers and readers alike?

Answering that question for myself: because I actively develop and deliver educational programs in book publishing, I am consistently in front of hundreds of students on an annual basis—a natural audience for a book like this. That is my awareness engine. I do not need to appeal to a broader trade audience because I am already directly appealing to my target audience: students that want to learn about publishing. If I do my job correctly, the reputation of my teachings and this book will percolate throughout this demographic, and this book will find its target audience.

This is the question you have to ask yourself when developing a title into a book. I encourage authors and publishers alike to consider these channels and explore them all simultaneously. As an author, you can develop books that could work well for trade distribution through traditional publishing means. You can develop books that could work well for the pervasiveness of digital distribution through these self publishing channels in tandem. It comes down to your goals and how you communicate with your readership.

All methods are valid. We are in a new era of unprecedented democratization—digital distribution can blast your work throughout the globe. This does not make the traditional trade gauntlet any less relevant, just different. Use this new era to your advantage.

INTELLECTUAL PROPERTY & RIGHTS

The facilitation of catalog, distribution, and print are deployed when a publisher is granted the **publishing rights** to a particular manuscript, or set of works, by the author via a publishing contract. Authors *always* retain the copyright of their work; a term that lasts 70 years upon publication. An author *never* signs away the copyright of their work, but rather grants a publisher a term to be the sole publisher of the work. This enables the publisher to exploit the works, generally for five to ten years, with options to renew the term via the book product the publisher creates.

Terms can vary and depend on a myriad of variables; cash advance, time left in the copyright, the market capabilities of the publisher, and so on.

If you look at a publishing company from a raw assets perspective, it's really an intellectual property company—a vehicle to exploit ideas. There are a myriad of avenues to do this beyond the print book product, particularly with the ever-blossoming field of digitization we've been discussing.

Audio rights, serializations, foreign rights, but perhaps most lucratively motion picture rights are some of the examples of rights publishers can obtain from authors when penning their publishing agreements. Each of these rights categories generally require additional incentives to the author—money upfront or revenue shares.

The optioning pipeline for motion picture rights is what I find most compelling—a powerful asset class. An option is when a film development company purchases the right to have the *option* to outright purchase and produce a piece of IP into a film or television program. The option typically lasts for one and a half to three years, before going up for re-negotiation. Sometimes a studio will keep renewing the IP purely to block other studios from having the option of production. As such, options in and of themselves could become compelling perennial assets.

Only 10% or so of what gets optioned gets produced. Outright acquisition and production opens up another deep array of profit corridors and opportunities for the author; writer or consultant credits, producer credits, upfront purchase fees, and—most succulently—residuals.

This is what comes to mind when I'm asked how Los Angeles is for book publishers.

III

REGARDING INFLUENCE &
THE INFLUENCER

The book business has not been kind to the influencer. Often writers that have built success through the vehicle of social media are unfairly relegated to a sort of artistic underclass. The crass titling of "Tumblr poet" used to refer to Rupi Kaur comes to mind, followed by the evolutions of "Instagram Poet," "BookToker," and so on down the chain of future social media platforms. This endless kaleidoscope of digital expression will surely provide original ways for writers to find new audiences, along with plenty of discrediting insults for legacy institutions to hurl at them.

But really, what makes an influencer any different from the editor of a publishing house? The job is curatorial production and distribution capital; *Hey, you, look at this. This is good. Trust in my taste when I tell you this is good.* Influencers who have grown to have exceptional careers generally sprawl freely from the confines of their original format—posting—into something far more broad and culturally impactful.

When considering this role of the influencer—curatorial taste—it is easy to see that the influencer holds a power that used to be exclusively gatekept by the book trade, the power to evoke and direct awareness. If the influencer is able to wield this lightning and bottle it up, does this make the publisher a vestigial apparatus?

It is not to say that the traditional publishing paths do not provide value to the influencer—recall the inner meetings of the trade and the power they have over determining what gets shelved and where—but this does give the influencer a great deal of opportunities to behave like their own publishing house utilizing the print-on-demand method of manufacturing and distribution detailed in the previous chapter.

Because the influencer is their own awareness vehicle, they solve for a vast majority of what the trade attempts to develop. Because print-on-demand has automated manufacturing, it has solved for a vast majority of what a publisher is responsible for in the productization of a book. If the influencer is able to provide the other missing pieces; compelling book design, tasteful editing, precise proofreading—the print-on-demand path could be a wildly competitive option to swiftly erect new works before a global audience, while capturing the entire pie chart of revenue generated from these self-published works.

As suggested in the Print on Demand section, it is useful to explore both traditional and self-publishing options in tandem, particularly if you are your own awareness vehicle. There is no reason not to deploy things that the trade may shy away from, or things that may speak to your whims at any given moment. The trade takes a long time to deploy a title (a minimum one year in advance). Whereas with self-publishing, you could upload your finished book files and see a title go live within weeks.

A clear downside is the quality and customization of the book as an object, but it is a perfect vehicle for simply designed perfect bound editions. Bringing back Rupi Kaur as my example; *Milk and Honey* was originally self-published using Amazon's KDP program. *Milk and Honey* found wild success driven by Rupi's own awareness engine and her pervasiveness on Tumblr and Instagram. Later, Andrews McMeel would come along and offer her a seven-figure advance to acquire the rights of the self-published work and obtain the rights to her future works.

Rather than one being superior to the other, the

self-publishing ecosystem and the traditional publishing world are complimentary. There are drawbacks and benefits to either path, but the supreme takeaway is that authors (both emerging talent and talent with their own awareness vehicles) no longer have to wait for the rubber stamp of a publisher to fully execute on a fleshed-out, fully realized book that emulates the bells and whistles of a trade release.

THE AWARENESS VEHICLE & MXF SCALE

Awareness is driven by two forms of fuel: authority and vibes. All individuals and companies dealing in an attention economy are contemplating this yin and yang of awareness. Authority largely encompasses education and entertainment; you know something, have something, that can be a value add to the person engaging with your content; be it knowledge, a portal to escape from the mundane, or even a new perspective for reverence in the mundane. Vibes are watery but no less objective—how do you want to make someone feel? Curating this sensation is an art that unpacks your own personal authority in necessary ways.

Leaning too far in one direction or the other can be fine in the short term, but is no way to strike perennial status. Authority without vibes comes off as cold, inaccessible, or arrogant: think of your least favorite teacher growing up or a stand-up comedian who turns against his audience.

Vibes without authority will eventually be read as superficial. Think of your favorite "junk food" TikTok content. TikTokers who are flashes in the pan seldom expand beyond the initial kernel that earned them views to begin with. They didn't find their voice, their authority, and were left in the churn.

Those who wish to capture awareness must be willing to wield authority. Those who wield authority must be able to command vibes. On paper, this sounds like a simple enough order of operations. The part that is subjective is what I like to call the **Mercurial X-Factor.**

The Mercurial X-Factor can be viewed as some kind of divine inspiration. It is a dense confluence of variables between space and time, a build-up of circumstances and skill that unlock an opportunity to thrust the package of authority and vibes into the larger zeitgeist. This is the answer to when someone asks, how did "this" become popular?

The Mercurial X-Factor can be lightning fast and

strike virality. But more often than not, the MXF gives the impression of great speed, but is in fact a slow, arduous process that is not discernable to the public.

Another way of describing the MXF is – it's what you bring to the table. It is the driving force behind what grants you authority and colors your vibes. The MXF is an amalgam of the countless hours you put into your craft, the people you know, the city you grew up in, the privilege you were born into, the thing that happened to you when you were five that indelibly changed your perspective. All of this pushes through the lens of where you are now in time, producing whatever it is you're producing. It is endless, it is shapeshifting, it cannot be pinned down. If you see it, you know it.

The MXF is the quiet magic beneath authority and vibes. It defies definition (just as authority and vibes defy definition). "You do you," in other words. The most objective throughline I have discovered in those who have strong MXF is twofold. It begins with honesty. They approach everything in their life with great integrity, and have a good sense for what does or doesn't work for them. They will do their best not to lie to their audience because most importantly, they will do their best not to lie to themselves.

The second part is enjoying the process; doing it for the love of the craft and making shit happen regardless of what platform or distribution or gate is "keeping you back." This should come as no surprise, but on the same hand, how many writers do we know that are writers simply in title? The difference between aspiration and application is the individual who enjoys the actual drudgery of doing the thing, and figures out a way of deploying their craft without any hint of external validation. Doing the thing is, of course, immensely hard. It's amazing anything gets done, ever. If you enjoy it, that is divine energy.

CONCERNING SCALE

Many young authors I have encountered are very concerned with the size of their audience. Growing their audience becomes the primary thrust of their labor in lieu of the craft that brought them to the table to begin with. It is easy to have comparison anxiety, to question why another's work is resonating (*MXF* (*Authority* + *Vibes*) = *Awareness*) while their own is not.

My perspective on audience is largely influenced by Ryan Holiday's *Perennial Seller*, a book you'll find in the Recommended Reading section of this book—a necessary text for those who wish to engage in the business of books, or content in general. This perspective is largely focused on the *quality* of the audience and not the *quantity*; the longevity of your content versus its widespread virality. Remember, the most efficacious viruses are not the most lethal; they are far more subtle, take their time, and adapt.

How do you find a quality audience? For starters, don't address the entire world. Get specific, find your niche. With a well-defined niche, the qualities that constitute MXF—truth and enjoyment of process—can flourish. This combination enables the individual to craft and express freely in their domain, establish authority and set a vibe.

I encourage reading Kevin Kelly's essay "1,000 True Fans" to fully appreciate this dynamic and to let go of any size fixation.

When it comes to art, scale should be a reaction to having discovered something that the world wants. It very rarely happens in the opposite direction.

BUILD

The most consistent throughline I have found in building audiences around books is the simple format of in-person events, either through workshops, readings, galas, or parties not even concerning any art. The very thing that drew me into the publishing world and launched my career was experiencing a *really good* poetry reading in a Long Beach bookstore on 4th Street called Open Books.

The reading was at the tail end of Derrick C. Brown's Poetry Revival tour. The featured readers that night were Anis Mojgani, Buddy Wakefield, Mindy Nettifee, and Derrick C. Brown himself. I was nineteen years old, post-highschool meandering, still in the process of really defining what mattered to me and how I wanted to apply myself. This reading cracked my mind open to the existence of today's American poetry. Throughout high school I was ruefully unaware that this realm of literature even existed, let alone a couple of cities away from where I grew up in Irvine.

What these poets did that night was present an expert combination of literary craft, sublime oration, and a *sick party*. Unlike the saccharine pageantry of slam poetry, these readers expressed something far deeper and true to their written works. It felt real, it felt punk, it felt cool. Derrick and his cohort of Write Bloody poets helped define the current wave of poetry we find ourselves in today, an increasingly popular genre by the numbers.

It wasn't long after this encounter in the Southern California poetry scene that I asked Derrick for a job. After a brief interview process at Write Bloody's downtown Long Beach office, he graciously provided this wayward but enthusiastic teenager with an internship. Being that it was just Derrick himself in the office, the internship quickly expanded in scope and responsibility as our two-man operation covered editorial, production, events, and fulfillment.

Two years later I knew it was time for me to make my way into Los Angeles proper, spurred on by a job opportunity at PEN America's Los Angeles chapter, which at the time was called PEN Center USA to reflect its distinct 501(c)(3) status from the New York office. I was brought on as the office's media and membership manager, handling public-facing communications, event production, as well as acting as a retainer unit for any membership shedding and keeping the top percentile of donors happy with personalized messages of gratitude and preferential invitations to our salons and readings.

In tandem to all of this I became a promoter for literary events in Los Angeles. I started a poetry series at Art Share LA called 'The Best,' largely because I felt LA needed better recursive reading programs and I wanted to have a vehicle I could offer all of my touring author colleagues that I met through Write

Bloody and PEN. The series consistently filled out the hundred-seat theater.

Through this program I met many of the active poets of the Los Angeles scene; Edwin Bodney, Alyesha Wise, Tonya Ingram, and Yesika Salgado. These poets would pack out audiences, and I noticed one crucial thing—none of them had books. From my experience with the Write Bloody poets, I knew that events were integral in moving the needle on book sales, and so when the opportunity came to start Not a Cult, my poetry imprint, these poets were the first to land on my frontlist.

I was not responsible for creating the audience these poets already had. Rather, I captured the energy they created and codified it in a curated list; I captured a scene. How did these poets create their audiences? Yesika Salgado wasn't always at influencer status with hundreds of thousands of followers.

What Yesika did, though, was engage with the Los Angeles community by creating events and participating in readings. Salgado was a member of LA's award-winning poetry slam team and created the open mic series Chingona Fire, opening up a platform where raw, emerging talent could work alongside more established writers at the trailhead of their careers. Salgado poured herself into cultivating this platform, and in turn, she created a die-hard local fanbase that seeded her popularity on Instagram, and soon after in mainstream media as her books picked up national attention.

If Salgado had not started by putting in the local attention in cultivating her audience I am certain her books would not have accelerated to national prominence the way they did. At least, not as quickly as they did. When we released her first title *Corazón* in 2016 we staged the book release event at the same venue where we had done our first readings together—Art Share LA. The venue far exceeded capacity, causing a panic among the on-site staff as we attempted to turn away audience goers, only to find that people were finding ways of circumventing the front entrance to sneak their way into the overly-packed theater.

I left PEN in 2013, obsessed with the idea of starting *my own thing*. In 2012, PEN had granted fiscal sponsorship to the fledgling Los Angeles Review of Books. As such, the start-up team for LARB was commonly in the PEN offices, and I got to watch as this motley crew of literary multi-hyphenates developed their concept for standing up a new company. I became close colleagues with the LARB founding team, and eventually quit PEN when one of them convinced me that I was wasting my time working at a nonprofit, that now's a good time to *fuck around and find out.*

There were a number of start-ups and failures between that and standing up Not a Cult. The press hit its stride early on because of that unique combination of timing, lessons learned from past failures, and the relationships built from the only "real" jobs I had carried previously.

For years, Not a Cult pushed out a series of hit events, bestselling books, and gained its fair share of successes. The throughline remained, as it does to this day, events—avenues where your readership can engage in a meaningful way is the core spirit of publishing in general. As authors you have to descend from the wizard tower, as publishers you have to open a door through the hedge. Invite people in, celebrate in the stories and discourse at hand.

I was lucky to receive opportunities to teach workshops and stand up educational programs in publishing, eventually developing the curriculum for the Los Angeles Review of Books Publisher's Workshop, a program targeting graduate students that want to begin their careers in book or magazine publishing. As such, this book exists, a reflection of years of teaching hundreds of students in real time as I've built the thing I teach about.

Knowing that building events, readings, workshops —however you want to engage an audience—is one of the most valuable things you can do for yourself and for and authorship, if you find yourself in a position where you've noticed that you're in a deficit of these kinds of programs, chances are you have to be the one to build them.

NOTES ON VALUE

In an age where we perceive the world as our audience through the vehicle of social media, it's important to remember that *it isn't*. As such, do not try to cater yourself to the world. If you try to appeal to everything you end up appealing to nothing.

There are innumerable ways to define value, but there is one keystone that rests at the heart of it, a perennial fountain of life. This is when the creator creates for themselves. The creator wants their creation to exist for few other reasons beyond their own personal fulfillment. Their passion and finesse will pour into this vessel and we are lucky for it to be shared with us. We get to participate in such a delicious function.

In other words, define value for yourself, let that extend into whatever it is you're doing. I basically just gave you all of Rick Rubin's book in two paragraphs, you're welcome.

BESTSELLER STATUS

Authors want bestseller status. It soothes the ego and we love it when numbers get bigger. It's a cool pip on the collar for sure. Yet it's hard to determine how bestseller status is even defined; it seems like there are a few other variables at play beyond raw sales. It's because there are a few other variables at play beyond raw sales. It's important to recall that such signifiers, while meaningful, are also vehicles for marketing and are not necessarily egalitarian. We point this out to break away from the comparative anxiety that such lists perpetuate. I will not, however, eschew the power of these rankings—they are significant as sales momentum begets sales momentum, and at the end of the day, I am pro-competition. As long as it's known *what* we're even competing in.

The Los Angeles & New York Times

The physical production of the book determines if a title is even eligible for bestseller status to begin with. Trade hardcovers are exclusively considered for the bestseller list in any genre category. *Paperbacks do not count.* The Big Five release titles, more often than not, with a hardcover edition followed by a paperback release a season or two after the hardcover. This happens primarily because there are better margins in hardcovers, and the avid fanbase will typically adopt the more expensive version in the presale and release season blitz. It's also a better archival edition for libraries.

Bestseller lists are then compiled on a weekly basis when an undisclosed aggregate of regional booksellers, some independent and some corporate (certain key Barnes & Noble locations, for instance), submit their weekly hardcover sales data to the editor responsible for producing bestseller lists. Ultimately it's something around a couple dozen selected booksellers that provide the data to create the lists.

So, yes, *The Times* lists do represent raw sales data, but only for a specific release format and only from a specific regional aggregate of brick-and-mortar shops.

Amazon

Amazon's bestseller list is represented by sales volume over time in its genre category. Amazon is perhaps the most impartial, democratic, and egalitarian to its sales rankings, fueled entirely by a title's rate of movement.

Not a Bestseller list, but related: Co-Ops

"Co-ops" are paid, premium positioning at bookstores or on online platforms. The best example of a "co-op" at a bookstore is at Barnes & Noble. If you see a central display of new releases or from a singular IP, this is likely a "co-op" table; publishers, via their distributor, pay a "co-op" fee for this placement.

Amazon has a similar functionality with certain front-page listings or pairings.

Very few independent booksellers do this because they have more skin in the game when it comes to their curatorial selections.

IV

COMPARISON OF NEW & LEGACY MODELS

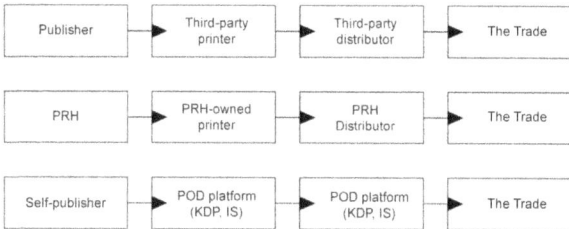

Publisher	Third-party printer	Third-party distributor	The Trade
PRH	PRH-owned printer	PRH Distributor	The Trade
Self-publisher	POD platform (KDP, IS)	POD platform (KDP, IS)	The Trade

A simple, modular chain: publishing company (content) —> printing company (manufacturing) —> distribution company (distribution) —> the trade (booksellers, etc.)

BIG FIVE & VERTICAL INTEGRATION

The book trade today is largely composed of five big media conglomerates. Bertelsmann owns Penguin Random House, News Corp owns HarperCollins, the private equity firm KKR owns Simon & Schuster, Holtzbrinck Publishing Group holds

MacMillan, and Hachette is under the Lagardère Group.

These multifaceted conglomerates own content, manufacturing, and distribution. Focusing on Penguin Random House as an example, they own printers that fulfill the manufacturing of their catalogs, and they own their own distribution company which also services the catalogs of other publishers that are not owned by them.

This vertical integration has a lot of upside when it comes to supply chain and reach, PRH is a combination of some of the largest publishing properties in the United States; as such, they hold many key and legacy relationships with the trade and continue regular, longstanding sales and trade conferences. When they want to print a title, they can tap one of the many offset or digital lines they own to rapidly deploy new products, warehouse their own inventory, and fulfill titles at advantageous rates within their own wholesale environment.

As mentioned, a publisher that is not owned by a Big Five publishing company can still be a client of a Big Five publishing company via distribution. One of Simon & Schuster's clients is the hip autofiction and scenester press Archway Editions. Archway started in 2020. Their frontlist was cutting-edge and picked up huge momentum with their sleekly designed, well produced books.

Baen Books, another S&S client, has a sprawling list of classic SciFi titles. As such, they get the benefit of S&S reps evangelizing their catalog to the trade, participating in S&S's thrice-a-year sales conference, and crucially they can deploy S&S printers at preferential rates to manufacture their print runs.

INDEPENDENT & THIRD PARTY PARTNERSHIPS

Publishers need to define their distribution and most do it through a third-party partnership with a distribution company (such as the scenario where a publisher not owned by a Big Five book publisher can still be a client of their distribution division). Anything outside of the Big Five is now mostly owned by Ingram, which we'll expand on shortly. There do remain a small handful of "independent" book distributors such as Southern California Book Distributors, Small Press Distributors, and the new Asterism Books which I will discuss in more detail later in this chapter.

But largely, the non-Big Five distribution arena is now under the umbrella of Ingram; Consortium,

Publishers Group West, Two Rivers, and the Perseus Book Group. This list constitutes over 1.5K publishers, about 35% of all new annual frontlist production.

Similar to the advantage of how Big Five distributors can utilize their vertically integrated print solutions, Ingram-owned distributors can utilize their robust print-on-demand grid to bridge gaps in, or entirely fulfill, supply chain for their titles. While the QA is lacking, the global agility of this solution is astounding and seems to be the only logical solution for a lot of low-volume print solutions, basically anything under 1,000 units.

If you're an independent publisher with a non-Ingram, non-Big Five owned distributor, you're left in a far more challenging position identifying where to print third-party and fulfill your distributor while maintaining a healthy margin, though sometimes low-volume scale makes sense for certain projects.

CONSIDERING THE SELF-PUBLISHER

So, if the world's largest eCommerce retail environment for books—Amazon—and the world's largest wholesaler of books—Ingram—can both be fulfilled with automated print-on-demand systems, where veritably every single sales channel that a trade distributor captures can be populated with digital listings of a print-on-demand objects, there's a serious fire under the ass of publishers and distributors to prove their value-add to individuals who may have significant personal distribution capital—celebrities, influencers, high net worth individuals, and so on.

A TANGENT REGARDING INGRAM

"Remember… with Ingram, the bookseller comes first."
— Ingram Book Co. slogan circa 1970

The Ingram family has a generational and diverse history of entrepreneurship in the United States. Prior to E. Bronson Ingram II founding the Ingram Book Company in 1970, his father Orrin Henry Ingram established successful businesses across lumber, oil refinement, and a network of inland distribution barges throughout the midwest. When Orrin Henry passed away in 1963, he left his two sons Bronson and Frederic the Ingram Oil & Refining Company, which they rebranded to the Ingram Corporation

In 1964, the Ingrams purchased the Tennessee Book Company, a textbook depository for the Tenenssee public schooling system. Simultaneous to Ingram's expansion to books, they acquired the Tennessee Insurance Company to become their own insurance provider across growing liabilities in physical assets across water and land.

The Ingrams continued to scale their business, diversifying into petroleum, chemicals, and the distribution of these related products using their inherited inland barge network. Despite their focus in energy industries, the books division displayed unexpected and rapid growth toward the end of the 1960s, prompting the rebranding of the Tennessee Book Company to the Ingram Book Company in 1970.

From the 1970s onward, the Ingram Book Company rolled out a series of industry-shifting programs; wildly competitive wholesale discounts for booksellers and unprecedented fulfillment speed in servicing the book trade on a national level, accelerated by warehouse acquisitions across the country. By 1980 the Ingram Book Company was the dominating wholesaler of books in the United States, a position they hold to this day.

To emphasize the Ingram Corporation's versatile and still-growing portfolio, E. Bronson Ingram II reorganized the corporate structure and rebranded the parent organization as Ingram Industries.

In 1981, the Ingram Book Company made its first move in diversifying beyond the wholesaling of books with the purchase of the John Yokley Company, its first commercial printer—a twinkle in the eye of today's print on demand.

In 1989 Ingram Industries acquired Micro D, which at the time was specialized in the distribution of personal computers; Micro D would become Ingram Micro, and Ingram Micro would go on to obtain a one-third market share in the distribution of information technology products and services. Ingram Micro has since spun off as its own corporate entity, siloed off from Ingram Industries.

E. Bronson Ingram II passed away in 1995 at the age of 63, and his two sons John and Orrin Ingram II became co-presidents of Ingram Industries. In 1997 under the direction of John Ingram, Lightning Print was developed to "print as few as one book at a time" to be a solution against the volume requirements of offset printing. By the end of 1998, Lightning Print had 1,500 books in its library. Today, what is now LightningSource receives 4,000 book uploads a day with a global print grid consisting of Ingram-owned printers across the US, UK, Europe, and Australia in addition to partnerships with regional printers in over twelve other countries covering six continents. (No print fulfillment in Antarctica… yet.)

"Why in the world are we wallpapering the warehouse with books? Wouldn't it be better to store a digital file and print a book when there was demand?"

— John Ingram

Ingram Industries now holds two subsidiaries that control their book interests, the Ingram Content Group and Ingram Publisher Services. This next part is remarkable to us in a contemporary context: in 2016, Ingram acquired Publishers Group West, Consortium Book Sales & Distribution, Perseus Distribution Services, Legato, and Perseus' digital asset management service Constellation. In a flourish, Ingram consolidated a significant portion of the "independent" book distribution field outside of the Big Five arena.

Today with John Ingram chairing the board of Ingram Industries, Ingram remains secure in its position as the de facto books wholesaler throughout the North American continent, with booksellers small and large primarily using iPage, Ingram's wholesale ordering tool, as their only method of acquiring inventory. Emerging e-commerce platforms such as Bookshop.org exclusively fill their orders via Ingram. With Ingram's network of digital printers, print-on-demand infrastructure, and consolidation of all major independent book distributors in the US, it is impossible to participate in the book trade without somehow participating with Ingram.

WHAT BECOMES VESTIGIAL

The primary current and future disruptions in the book trade rest in distribution. This is contrary to lay readers' belief that eBooks and digitization are the primary cause of disruption in books. The big shift has been distribution. A crucial and perhaps obvious example of this is the advent of "big eCommerce"—Amazon—which has largely impacted independent brick-and-mortar book-sellers, but has also sent a ripple effect through wholesale and distribution environments.

Amazon holds a very unique position in the book trade. Any account-holder with a distributor can negotiate their wholesale rate based on a number of variables—primarily purchasing power. Generally "indie" accounts just signing up to a service such as Ingram's iPage or any distributor gets a fresh 30%-40% wholesale discount. Accounts negotiate on an annual basis for increasingly preferential rates. A recent example of this is when Barnes & Noble saw their wholesale discount rise from 50% to 52% after being negotiated down from their original bid of an increase to 55%.

The account holder with the largest discount in the book trade is Amazon, with a 55% wholesale discount. This preferential treatment is twofold; one part artifact and one part leverage. The artifact is Amazon received preferential rates back when they were a scrappy bookselling start-up with the novel idea of fulfilling purchases through the internet. Now, it's rare to see trade-distributed accounts that don't have Amazon comprising *at least half* of all of their trade sales.

This begs an interesting question: if the majority of trade sales are now occurring through Amazon, what is the use of a distributor to the book trade? The margins in wholesaling books are already delicate; with a 55% discount, 20-28% distributor fees, plus a deep array of co-op, storage, freight, and other miscellaneous fees that get layered onto publisher accounts, some publishers see cents per unit returning on their wholesales to Amazon.

The original function of distributors is the oldest legacy function of all—relationships! During seasonal sales conferences, reps from all sides of the trade get together and make a case for their catalogs. There are far fewer booksellers now, making it all the more important to cultivate relationships with those that remain.

This original function seems to have been over-ridden by the low-hanging fruit of the eCommerce giant, filling the furnace of an ever-churning, easily accessible content grab. There is no rep to appeal to Amazon. There is no storefront; instead, an algorithmic current and ease of access. There is no human appeal. So, again, why would one need a distributor to leverage the sales channel of Amazon?

Asterism Books responds to this question in a compelling way, and perhaps a way that's indicative of the future. Asterism is one of the few new distributors to the book trade to emerge in the last twenty years. It's a field lacking—but in desperate need of—fresh, younger generational competition.

Asterism recognizes the unique challenges of the digital landscape and offers non-exclusive distribution contracts. The value-add they provide is that they host a network of relationships—that *original function*—of over two hundred independent booksellers that receive their catalog. They make their titles available to this closed-network trade, and leave more extraneous activities up to the publisher; such as filling Amazon *direct*.

The publisher is free to make their own seller's account with Amazon and fulfill their purchases either by Fulfilled By Amazon (FBA, which enables Prime) or by fulfilling Amazon purchases themselves. The FBA option is a monthly subscription something to the tune of $30.00, plus a 30% take off of the net price. That 30% off a full retail list price is far more competitive than the margin a publisher earns after a maximum 55% discount plus the distributor fee ranging around 25%. If a publisher is to opt into the ease of accessibility of Amazon, non-exclusivity with a distributor seems to be the most solvent option.

Furthermore, publishers in control of their own digital catalog separate from their distributors can benefit from Amazon's robust distribution network for eBooks by simply uploading their digital e-titles to KDP (while using IngramSpark in tandem with this for total global and platform coverage). Otherwise, eBooks are subject to the same wholesale discounts and distributor fees if pushed through normal trade distribution circuits.

I can readily see a future where publishers unionize within their respective distribution groups to elect for non-exclusivity when it comes to accounts like Amazon for print formats, and completely divest for digital formats. Or at least appeal for diminished distributor fees when it comes to these accounts that do not receive human intervention for their sales aptitude.

LITERARY AGENTS

The literary agent makes their living from the upfront capital made in advances and rights purchases. Where does the literary agent stand in today's risk-averse, saturated content market where advances have diminished across the board? There remain some staunch independent agents apart from legacy Manhattan firms with solid relationships with the Big Five, but otherwise the literary agent pool has largely been consolidated under Creative Artists Agency (CAA) and William Morris Endeavor (WME).

It stands to reason that the big talent firms of Los Angeles would control a meaningful segment of literary talent—the bedrock of IP and motion picture rights licensing. Advance behavior nowadays is pointed toward the least risky venture, in other words, established talent with proven distribution capital. This consolidated landscape, like many other dynamics occurring in the trade, makes it more difficult for emerging talent attempting to break in—and more difficult for established talent to negotiate.

The other end of the spectrum is the boutique literary agent; generally a solo business, an individual who has longstanding legacy relationships with an authorship and publishers. From what I've observed, these are typically treated as passion projects and less as meaningful business endeavors.

V

THE FUTURE

HYBRIDIZATION

Amid the current wave of digital disruption, there are categories of authors that can steward their own distribution capital toward the propagation of their titles. In other words, they can invest in their own books, fully release their own titles at the same level as the book trade, and reap the benefits of controlling their own catalog across IP ownership, rights licensing, and maintaining a majority (or total) share of their revenues. A publisher has to step up as *more* than a middleman, which they can do by providing competitive editorial and distribution services that exceed the quality of what print on demand and its associated digital distribution channels can offer.

The pay-to-play "vanity press" has a long and lurid history of snake oil salesmanship. Under this model, the author provides all of the required capital to produce, print, and distribute their book. This side of the industry is packed with grifters, capturing the dream of being a *published author* and over-promising on the vision of what the process entails. Today, many iterations of the "vanity press" simply offer the automated print-on-demand solutions that have been detailed in this book, yet dress it up as if they are providing some unique gate-kept distribution solution. Do not be fooled.

However, there is something to be said about the author-financed model and compelling ways that co-investment and ownership can be examined in a "hybrid" publishing environment; something I am convinced is the publishing model of the future. Given that competitive talent with high distribution capital can simply self-publish their work, distribute it globally, and open up a meaningful revenue stream for themselves; why not pay for a professional team to handle the aspects of editorial and distribution—particularly if that distribution is not exclusive to the quality confines of print-on-demand?

If a publisher curates their frontlist with the same integrity as the titles they're investing in, but offers levers on how their publishing contracts behave insofar as financing, revenue splits, and ownership, there is compelling room for growth and deal flow that can provide authors who contain far greater distribution capital than the publisher for both parties to maximize value to the other.

I am *not* saying that it's a good model for a publisher to accept paying clients freely. There should be the same deep layer of scrutiny applied to authors who pay for their projects as there is toward projects that the publisher is investing in; the same curatorial value which would make facilitation into trade distribution meaningful.

What would these levers look like? On a contractual level, a few key variables can fluctuate depending on the source of capitalization for any given project. With a traditional publishing contract where the publisher is acquiring the publishing rights to a manuscript, the total capital expectation is on the publisher—there's an advance, a budget for marketing, the author receives a 10-20% royalty, and any other rights licensing split is negotiated.

A hybrid publishing contract still grants the publishing rights to the publisher, but perhaps on a more strict term. The total capitalization is passed on to the author with an added fee for editorial services (basically an advance but in reverse, paid to the publisher), but the author receives the majority of the royalty, licensing share, and other profits generated from the work.

This arrangement requires great transparency, financial modeling, and planning on the part of the publisher to ensure that the plan actually has a shot at a return, as the author is shouldering a great deal of risk typically absorbed by the publisher.

As such, the authors that would be viable candidates for such a process are *extremely specific*. They are capitalized, both financially as well as with distribution potential; ultimately their IP is worth more to them if they retain it in-house. They are their own imprint unto themselves. This particular type of author is still selected like any frontlist candidate would be, but the balance of power has shifted and has outpaced the speed that traditional publishing works at.

Some of these hybrid-model candidates could still be captured in the traditional publishing sense if provided with a massive advance figure. However, this "hybrid" model affords publishing houses the ability to finance their catalogs much like a film studio finances their film slates; from a consortium of investors or capitalized talent (executive producers) that benefit far more directly from the return on investment of the mass-distributed product.

THE PART I WILL READ AT READINGS

An essential task for the career author is to hone in the oration of their own work. Reading out loud to an audience at a bookstore, or any function that otherwise incorporates sharing work, is a core and accessible component to creating an audience around your work.

When I say accessible, I mean it is a muscle, one that can be worked out and refined like any other part of your body. Anyone can do this given the practice and discipline. If you are not good at reading in front of an audience, keep reading in front of audiences until you are. The feeling of discomfort and social adrenaline will never go away, but eventually, you will know what dropping into your own vocal command feels like.

I have been going to readings since I was a teenager. Having taken in a great range and aesthetic variety of reading, I have developed an appreciation for curating an optimized reading format. Something that achieves the following:

A) The audience does not begin to stir. The run of show is dialed in and specific. Nothing meanders. The talent knows their time, their pacing, and selects excerpts or dialogue that is precise and leaves the audience wanting more. I have found this run of show to not exceed 60 minutes of total allotted time across readers or programmatic elements.

B) There is an amiable pre and post show with music and normal party selections; drinks, a second location within the location, a place to smoke, good mellow lighting (tough to find in bookstores), and an accessible route for an afterparty. Bonus points if the venue can host an after party.

C) Generally enter an event space knowing that people are there mostly to talk to other people. The reading component is cool and important, and is a unifying aesthetic for everyone to participate in. It is celebratory, but remember not to hold anyone hostage to the whims of an unorganized spotlight.

To summarize, do not waste people's time. If you are talent, respect not going over time. If you are a promoter, respect the talent's time by providing a succinct vessel with a defined run-of-show. Remember that time moves faster on a stage but stays the same for an audience, so slow down, move intentionally, and breathe. In other words, take your time, but don't steal theirs.

The spoken word commands a power of indoctrinating influence unlike any other medium, even more so than the written word. Speakers can and do change the course of individual lives. This scales with certain vehicles, such as religion and books.

The key institution behind any memetic happening or popularity is a cool event. If you can activate the fundamental human impulse of gathering together for a shared purpose, and if you make this activation quality and worthy of the audience's time, you have done nothing short of wielding the fundamental lifeblood of cultural movement.

It is a hugely influential activity. The repetitive behavior I have observed across every cultural industry—be it the art, literary, or Hollywood worlds—is that, at the end of the day, all we really want to do is hang out in a cool space with people we admire, be seen, heard, and celebrated, and share equally in that exuberance with our colleagues.

Thank you for being here with me throughout the journey of this book, hearing my words, and partic-ipating with my expression.

BIBLIO OPTIMISM, AN AFTERWORD

It is true that the landscape of books has changed dramatically in the last decade. It is true there are fewer bookstores, that the independent bookseller is uncomfortably squeezed by hegemonic eCommerce giants—it is true that there are fewer risks being taken on emerging talent, that advances have dried up across big and small publishers alike—it is true that finding a job in publishing seems as much of a lark as being able to be a full time writer. It is true that the age of information and the accelerated speed of our technologies has added complex variables to overcome in a slow moving, legacy medium.

This all may make one feel hopeless in the midst of a low-retention attention economy where minds flock and scatter like an impetuous cloud of pigeons. Content plays fast and loose, depth is a luxury afforded to those who have an abundance of time to really sit back and cogitate.

Reader, books will endure. That's what they do. That's why we made them. No genre is dead, but like any living thing, we're in a constant entropic and rebirthing process; ebbs and flows, golden and dark ages. Do not be fooled by solipsistic gestures spouted by pitiful old souls yearning for a time that is behind us. These shallow takes lack a perspective of history and a true lust for craft. Those who are hungry and interested will think about the reader of tomorrow, not of ships long departed from harbor. Celebrate what was and acknowledge where we are now, and think about the glory to be stewarded ahead.

Endurance requires change, and the very fundamental function of a publisher is changing. The democratization of publishing and the awareness power of the individual has fundamentally disrupted the systems previously exclusive to the publisher. An example of this is when Elon Musk posts a Tweet, he is a publisher; his published works can influence entire markets. This poses a massive challenge to legacy media, but provides great opportunity for those who can figure out how to combine what worked in the old model—curation, refinement— with what is pervasive in the new model—a wealth of rapid attention.

Books require precision, and the art of precision— editing, good design, elegant productization— remains a throughline between the past and present of books. Individual authors can now deploy teams to facilitate these roles, indistinguishable from a publishing house and without the bloat of administration. If the individual author has more distribution capital than the publisher, the individual author is the publisher.

Print-on-demand technologies will become increasingly sophisticated. I have seen the quality and customizable options blossom from 2010-2020. Year after year we will see growing improvements to the system, and Ingram's continued monopolistic grip on this new era of service to the book trade. Distributors have already been greatly consolidated under Ingram, and the amount of independent book distributors that exist outside of any Big Five or Ingram environment, you can count on one hand. I am interested in seeing what Asterism books does; they are the one new book distributor to have emerged in the last decade. Creating new vehicles of distribution is an area that can be disrupted, though it is a momentous task to compete against e-commerce giants and a narrowing pool of independent booksellers.

With that being said, the publisher as we know it will not go entirely extinct because there is still the vital role of evangelizing new talent. The editor who diligently reads through slush piles, attends conferences, goes to readings, and finds the next great manuscript that needs attention. These intrepid risk-takers will discover the next great IP, the next great unobvious thing. This is where the spirit and adventure of publishing exists; immersing oneself into an unknown field of letters, emerging from it with books underarm.

How do we adapt to the times? The cunning publisher will integrate POD technologies to keep their backlist eternally active regardless of demand, relinquishing warehousing restraints, automating supply chains and keeping a historic archive of their lists active forever. This idea excites me, even if it grants far more power toward Ingram's book cloud and print grid. This path incentivizes working with a distributor owned by Ingram, or cutting out third party distribution entirely in favor of using an Ingram platform like LightningSource to facilitate digitized trade distribution.

The cunning author will not wait for a publisher to make them whole. This advice goes for any creative, but especially the writer—in this era of democratized distribution, *do not wait for anything*. Make, and make, and make—publish, and publish, and publish. If the right opportunity comes along for you to partner with a literary agent or sell your manuscript to a publisher, of course explore that— and I hope the words in this book help you discern if that relationship would be valuable or not. But otherwise, deploy. The industry's attention has sped up alongside the attention of readers; waiting for platforms means you are already dead in the water. Assume the mantle, behave like the platform, and operate at the level of gatekeepers. This will give you a better chance at building an audience independent of publishers, and will give you better leverage when working with publishers.

That is, ultimately, the soul of this book. The entire appeal I am trying to make here is that there is nothing stopping you from writing a book and publishing it at a global level. Gone are the days of waiting for something to happen to you—to happen to your work. Today you have to be a confluence of vision and application. The pure visionaries are too slow, bless their hearts. Let's put them in a think tank. The independent writers of today have to *apply* their vision—and amazingly, in the last decade, they now have the tools to do just that.

While this may be oxymoronic, do not relinquish precision for speed. Still apply a layer of quality on what you are publishing—take editing seriously. Find collaborators you trust who will marshal your untethered meandering aspects into an unforgettable text. The reader of tomorrow wants to find depth but needs that precise direction to get hooked. This theory is validated by witnessing how poetry as a genre has seen 10-15% annual growth in unit sales from 2015-2020. TikTok has accelerated precise bites that hook young minds into exploring new niches. This has stoked growth in poetry, essay collections, and short story anthologies—genres the trade were generally allergic to prior to 2016.

Don't forget that the book market is still a 140 billion dollar industry. At the end of the day, literature remains the bedrock of all content. Book publishers are, really, IP companies. Licensing and subrights remain lucrative perennial profit corridors for the discerning publisher. Anyone who works in books who is apathetic or lazy about making money, be wary of them, as this sentiment creates a predestined vacuum.

The artist should be well compensated for their works, and authors publishing their writing should treat their published works like the portfolio of assets that they are. You want to create diverse holdings, and you want to make sure if you are signing away the rights of your assets, that you trust the stewardship of that asset—that they will grow value for it in ways you otherwise couldn't have without the strategic partnership.

While the days of lifestyle-sustaining advances are (mostly) gone, direct sales and independent audience development can supplement the independent's cashflow. It requires a layer of future-thinking and use of today's technologies to deploy products, services, or programs that directly benefit the independent. If the independent is able to create an audience, they have subverted the very need for a publisher to begin with and, ironically, gained more leverage with the institutions. The money hasn't left the industry, its priorities have simply changed.

If you use those changes to propel you forward rather than fighting against them, then there is no better time than now to be part of the book trade.

GLOSSARY

Catalog
A comprehensive list of books available from a publisher, often organized by season or genre, and used to showcase their offerings to buyers, bookstores, libraries, and other stakeholders.

Frontlist
The selection of a publisher's newest titles, typically those released within the current or most recent publishing season, which are the focus of active marketing and promotion efforts.

Backlist
The collection of a publisher's older titles, which are no longer actively promoted as new but continue to be sold and generate revenue over time.

The Book Trade
The collective ecosystem of publishers, distributors, wholesalers, booksellers, and other entities involved in the production, distribution, and sale of books to readers.

Trade Distributor / Trade Distribution
An organization or service that acts as a middleman between publishers and retailers (or libraries), handling warehousing, order fulfillment, and shipping of books to various sales channels.

Sales Channel
A means through which books reach their final consumers, including bookstores (brick-and-mortar and online), libraries, wholesale markets, and direct sales from publishers or authors.

Wholesaler
A company that buys books in bulk from publishers or distributors and resells them to bookstores, libraries, and other retailers at a discount.

Publication Date
The official release date of a book, when it becomes available for sale to the public through various sales channels.

Ship Date
The date on which a book is physically shipped from the publisher, printer, or distributor to retailers, wholesalers, or libraries. This often precedes the official publication date to ensure that books are available on shelves or in warehouses when the title officially launches.

Distribution Capital

When I use the term distribution capital with authors, I mean the author's native ability to generate an awareness campaign around their own work. This can be in the form of social media or any form of celebrity. When I use the term distribution capital with publishers, I mean their ability to develop prestige and build an audience around their curatorial tastemaking. Today, authors sometimes are more competitive than their publishers in terms of distribution capital.

Offset Printing

A traditional printing method where an inked image is transferred (or "offset") from a metal plate to a rubber blanket, then onto the printing surface. This technique is cost-effective for large print runs due to its high quality and low per-unit cost at scale.

Digital Printing

A modern printing method that uses digital files (like PDFs) to produce books directly, without the need for physical plates. Ideal for short print runs, quick turnaround times, and customization.

Print on Demand (POD)

A publishing and printing model where individual copies of a book are printed only when an order is placed, reducing the need for inventory and minimizing upfront costs.

Amazon KDP (Kindle Direct Publishing)
Amazon's self-publishing platform that allows authors and publishers to publish and distribute eBooks and print-on-demand paperbacks globally, offering a range of tools for marketing and sales tracking.

IngramSpark / Lightning Source
A division of Ingram Content Group that provides self-publishing and print-on-demand services for independent authors and publishers, offering global distribution to retailers and libraries.

Mercurial X-Factor
An unseeable quality, typically a combination of qualities, that create a unique characteristic in a person that takes them or their work from "good" to "great."

Ingram
The largest book wholesaler in the world as well as one of the largest book distributors in the world, serving as a critical link between publishers and booksellers, libraries, and other retailers by providing warehousing, logistics, and fulfillment services.

Ingram's iPage
An online ordering and account management platform for booksellers and libraries, offering access to Ingram's extensive catalog, including book availability, pricing, and ordering tools.

Edelweiss+
A web-based platform used by publishers, booksellers, librarians, and reviewers for catalog browsing, title discovery, and advanced title marketing. It includes tools for managing book reviews, sales pitches, and inventory planning.

RECOMMENDED READING

Book Business by Jason Epstein (W.W. Norton & Company, 2001)
ISBN: 978-0393321784

Perennial Seller by Ryan Holiday (Portfolio / Penguin Random House, 2017)
ISBN: 978-0143109013

ABOUT

Daniel Lisi is a publisher, writer, and producer from Newport Beach, California. He is the founder and publisher of Not a Cult, a press dedicated to poetry and art, and Network Press, focused on concepts for the future. Lisi has been a key member on the founding teams of multiple media startups and has overseen the development of various publishing ventures from seed-stage to self-sufficiency.

www.ingramcontent.com/pod-product-compliance
Lightning Source LLC
Chambersburg PA
CBHW030530210326
41597CB00014B/1089